St. Linus

The Discovery Books are prepared

under the educational supervision of

Mary C. Austin, Ed.D.

Reading Specialist

and Lecturer on Education

Harvard University

A DISCOVERY BOOK

by Charles P. Graves

illustrated by Gerald McCann

GARRARD PUBLISHING COMPANY
CHAMPAIGN, ILLINOIS

Benjamin Franklin

Man of Ideas

For Liz, Liza, and Johnny

Contents

Benjamin Franklin: Man of Ideas

Chapter *1*

The Swimming Machine

"I've invented a swimming machine," twelve-year-old Ben Franklin shouted. "Come indoors and see it."

Ben was leaning out of a window of his family's house in Boston. He was talking to his friend, Tom Eliot, who stood in the street below. The year was 1718. Tom had a kite under his arm. He was planning to fly it. But he was curious about Ben's swimming machine.

Tom came into the house. Ben showed him two wooden boards. The boards were about a foot long and six inches wide. Each board had a small hole in the middle.

"That doesn't look like a machine to me," Tom said.

"Well, maybe it isn't a machine," Ben admitted. "But I bet these boards will help me swim faster. I'll put my thumbs through these holes and use the boards as paddles."

"Have you tried them out yet?" Tom asked.

"Let's go to the pond and try them now," Ben cried. "Come on!" The two boys ran out of the house.

When they reached the pond, they took off their clothes.

"We'll race to that rock out there," Ben said. He pointed to a big stone about a hundred yards from shore. "One! Two! Three! Go!"

The boys jumped into the water. Because of the boards on his hands, Ben made a big splash.

At first Ben was clumsy. Tom pulled ahead. But soon Ben learned how to use the boards properly. He came up even with Tom. Then he splashed ahead. Ben won by about ten yards.

"I knew my swimming machine would work," Ben boasted.

"It sure does," Tom agreed. "And you sure do have good ideas."

"I have another idea," Ben said. "Let's fly your kite and I'll show you."

The boys swam back to shore. They got the kite flying high in the air. Ben wound the kite string around his hand. Then he jumped into the pond. When he came up he floated on his back.

As the kite was blown by the wind, it pulled Ben through the water. It was lots of fun.

"Hey," Ben yelled to his friend. "I feel like a sailboat. Better bring my clothes over to the other side."

While Ben was dressing Tom said, "Ben, you have more ideas than any other boy in Boston. Some of them may be crazy. But a lot of them are good, too."

"Oh!" Ben cried. "There are millions of ideas that haven't even been thought of yet."

"Well, I'm sure you will think of lots of them," Tom said. Tom was certainly right. Benjamin Franklin had good ideas all his life.

Chapter *2*

Candle Beams

When Ben came home it was suppertime. His mother had just finished cooking in the big fireplace. His father and his many brothers and sisters were sitting at the table.

Ben's father looked up. "Have you been wasting time again watching the ships come in?"

"Not today, Father," Ben answered. "But I don't call watching ships a waste of time. You know I want to be a sailor when I grow up. I want to go everywhere and see everything."

"No, Ben," Mr. Franklin said. "I have told you before. You're meant for something better than the sea. You have a good mind. I am sorry I had to take you out of school. But I just did not have the money to keep you there."

Ben had been born in Massachusetts in 1706. Massachusetts belonged to England then. It was one of the young American colonies. There weren't many schools in the colonies. But Ben was luckier than most boys. He went to school for two years. After that he studied at home.

Ben also helped his father in his business. His father made candles to sell to the people of Boston. Ben heated the candle wax and poured it into the molds.

"I know you don't like working for me," Mr. Franklin once said to Ben. "Most boys don't like working for their fathers."

"It's not that," Ben said quickly. "I don't like making candles. I want to do something more important."

"You think making candles is not important?" Mr. Franklin cried. "Without candles, how could people see at night? How could they read?"

He pointed to a candle burning brightly on a table. " 'How far that little candle throws his beams,' " he said proudly. " 'So shines a good deed in a naughty world.' "

"That's good, that's good!" Ben clapped his hands. "Did you make that up?"

"No. A famous writer named Shakespeare did."

"I wish I could write things like that," Ben said.

His father smiled. "You know, Ben, you have always liked words and sayings. Maybe you should work with words. Your brother James may need a boy in his printing shop."

"I think I would like printing, Father," Ben said. "And I just had an idea. Making candles *is* important. If you don't keep on making candles, how can people read the things I'm going to print?"

"Well said, young man," his father cried. "We will go to see James tomorrow."

Chapter *3*

"Silence Dogood"

When Ben was growing up, boys learned a business by becoming apprentices. An apprentice agreed to work for a certain number of years without pay. In return, the man he worked for taught him a business. An apprentice lived with his master and got free meals.

Mr. Franklin took Ben to see James at his printing shop.

"Good morning, James," Mr. Franklin said. "I wonder if you need an apprentice. I mean Ben."

"I do need a boy," James answered. "But remember this. I won't be easy on Ben just because he is my brother."

"I don't want any favors," Ben said. "I want to learn the printing business."

Ben promised to work for his brother until he was twenty-one. From the very first day, he liked the printing business. It was fun spelling out words with the metal letters, or type. And it was even more fun to ink the type and see the words printed on paper.

But James was not kind to Ben. He often scolded him. He was jealous because Ben learned so quickly.

James was pleased, however, when Ben thought of a money-saving idea.

"Give me half the money you pay for my meals," Ben told James. "I will feed myself and you can save the rest."

Ben's idea made James happy. And Ben was happy too. He often made a whole meal out of a slice of bread and a handful of raisins. He spent only half the money James gave him for food. The money he saved he spent on books. When Ben finished reading one book, he sold it. Then he bought another book.

James printed a newspaper called *The New England Courant*. One day Ben said, "James, I would like to write a story for the newspaper."

"Ha, ha!" James laughed. "You are much too young. Who would want to read anything you wrote?"

Ben's feelings were hurt. He thought he was a pretty good writer. He had a friend, John Collins, who was an apprentice in a bookstore. Ben often wrote stories and read them to John. John always liked what Ben wrote.

"Why don't you play a trick on James?" John suggested later. "Write a story and make James think a grownup wrote it."

"That's a good idea," Ben said. "And you know how I like good ideas!"

There were no typewriters in those days. Everything had to be written by hand. Ben wrote a story. He changed his handwriting so James would not know it was his. To fool James even more, he signed the story "Silence Dogood".

Late that night Ben slipped the story under the door of the printing shop. The next morning James found the story.

"This is good," James shouted. "Mighty good! I wonder who wrote it. I'm sure it was an important man!"

Ben almost laughed out loud.

"Here, Ben," James said, handing him the story. "We will print this in the next copy of the *Courant*."

That was one copy Ben really enjoyed printing. When people read his story, they liked it and asked for more. So Ben kept on writing. The readers tried to guess who "Silence Dogood" really was. They knew it was a made-up name. But nobody guessed a boy like Ben could write so well.

One day Ben proudly told James that he was "Silence Dogood".

"You!" his brother cried. "I don't believe it. The stories are not written in your handwriting."

"I changed my writing so you wouldn't guess," Ben explained.

Then James knew that Ben was a better writer than he was. James was even more jealous than before. He did not like having a younger brother so smart.

James became harder and harder to work for. Nothing Ben did pleased him. James often got angry for no reason at all. He beat Ben with a stick. Ben decided he could not work for James any longer.

He knew he would have to leave Boston. He had promised to work for James until he was twenty-one. If he broke his word, James could keep him from getting another job in Boston. He might even have Ben arrested.

John Collins agreed to help Ben escape. He found a ship that was sailing for New York. Ben had to sell some of his precious books to pay for the trip. Late one night he crept onto the ship.

When Ben awoke the next morning the ship was far out to sea. Ben was just seventeen. He had no friends in New York. And he had very little money in his pockets. But he had many good ideas in his head. And good ideas are often worth lots of money.

Chapter *4*

On His Own

Ben could not find a printing job in New York. He soon found that he had almost no money left.

"Maybe I should go back home," he said to himself. But he knew he would feel like a failure if he did.

Someone told Ben he might find a printing job in Philadelphia. Ben thought his problems over carefully.

"What have I got to lose?" he laughed. He felt the few coins still in his pockets. Then he started for Philadelphia.

First he took a boat to New Jersey. Then he started hiking. He walked fifty miles in the rain. When he reached the Delaware River, he found a rowboat that was going to Philadelphia. Ben climbed in and helped row.

Here is the way Ben described his arrival in the city where he was to become famous:

"I was dirty from my journey. My pockets were stuffed out with shirts and stockings. And I knew no soul nor where to look for lodging. I was fatigued with traveling, rowing and want of rest. I was very hungry and my whole stock of cash consisted of a Dutch dollar and about a shilling in copper."

Ben was so tired that he went into a church and fell asleep.

When he awoke, he found a room at a hotel. Ben was hungry. He was glad when dinner was ready.

While he was eating, one of the men at his table asked, "Where are you from, young fellow?"

"Boston," Ben answered.

"What are you doing so far from home?"

Ben was upset. "This man may guess I'm a runaway apprentice," he thought. "He might send me home."

Ben knew he must say something quickly. "You see, sir," he explained, "I learned the printing trade in Boston. But I couldn't get a job there or in New York. So I have come to Philadelphia to make my living."

The man seemed satisfied. "Well, good luck, my boy," he said. "I'm sure you will succeed."

The man was right. Ben got a job with a Philadelphia printer almost at once. The next few years were full of adventure. Ben took a trip on a sailing ship to London. He worked there as a printer for eighteen months.

Then Ben returned to Philadelphia. He and a friend started their own printing shop. It was a great success. Ben also bought a newspaper. He made it the best paper in all the colonies.

Now that Ben was making money, he decided he should marry. *"A single man,"* he said, *"is like the odd half of a pair of scissors."*

When Ben first came to Philadelphia, he had met a girl named Deborah Read. He had been in love with her a long time. Now he and "Debbie" were married.

Debbie was a good wife. She made Ben's clothes. And she helped in the printing shop. She folded the pages and sewed them together to make books. Debbie helped Ben save money. He was proud of her.

Debbie was also busy taking care of the baby, William. When little Francis was born, Ben and Debbie were happy. Now William had a playmate.

In those days many children died of smallpox. Debbie was planning to have Francis inoculated against the disease.

But the doctor thought she should wait until Francis was stronger.

That was a terrible mistake. One night Debbie and Ben were awakened by loud crying. It was Francis. They felt his forehead. It was very hot.

Ben went for the doctor. But it was too late. Little Francis had smallpox. In a few days he was dead.

Debbie and Ben were heartbroken. They didn't have another baby for many years. But when Sally arrived, she was a great joy.

When Sally was six, Ben wrote about her to his mother.

"Sally is a good little girl," he said. "She minds her parents. We are sending her to dancing school."

Ben also told his mother that when he died he hoped people would say that *"he lived usefully"*. He didn't want them to say *"he died rich"*.

Ben certainly lived usefully. But his many good ideas were making him rich.

Chapter 5

Trying Everything

Benjamin Franklin made a success of nearly everything he tried. And he tried nearly everything. He published a yearly magazine called *Poor Richard's Almanac.* It contained something of interest to nearly everyone. Farmers liked the weather reports. Sailors liked the news about the tides. Women read the cooking lessons. And children enjoyed the poems.

Poor Richard's Almanac became famous for the wise sayings in it.

Among them were:

"Eat to live; not live to eat."

"Early to bed and early to rise makes a man healthy, wealthy and wise."

Ben made up some of the sayings himself. But he took most of them from the writings of other wise men. He often changed the words so people could understand them better.

Ben and some of his friends started a club called the Junto. The members liked to swap ideas. And they also liked to swap books. They helped start the first public library in Philadelphia.

The club members studied many different things. They talked about them at the meetings.

At that time America was ruled by the king of England. One night Ben asked the club a question. "If a king tries to take away the rights of a man, does the man have a right to resist?"

It was a hard question to answer. Many people thought a king could do no wrong.

Another member of the club stood up. "I think a man should fight for his rights," he said, "even if he has to fight a king."

"Before he fought," Ben said quietly, "wouldn't it be wiser to talk with the king? Even a king should listen to reason."

Ben did not know it at the time, but the question they were talking about would fill his thoughts for many years.

When the Junto meeting came to an end, Ben started for home. It was a dark night. There were no street lights in Philadelphia.

As Ben was crossing a street, he tripped on a piece of firewood someone had dropped. Ben went sprawling into a mud puddle.

Debbie hardly knew him when he reached home.

"It's me, Ben," he said, wiping the mud from his face.

"Your suit is ruined!" Debbie said.

"I'm lucky I didn't break my leg," Ben replied. "The streets are not safe at night. Something must be done."

Ben saw that something was done. He got Philadelphia to light the streets at night. And he arranged to have the streets swept clean. "Maybe it's a good thing for other people that I fell in that mud puddle!" he told Debbie.

And that wasn't all Ben did. He helped start the city's first fire department and the first hospital.

Ben was certainly busy. Yet when he had "time off", he invented things. One of his most famous inventions was the Franklin Stove. In those days, houses were very cold in winter for there were no furnaces. And much of the fireplace heat went up the chimney. Ben hated to see Debbie and his children shivering. So he invented a stove which fitted in the fireplace. It sent heat out into the room. Soon many families had Franklin stoves to keep them warm.

Ben would not take any money for his invention of the stove. "I use inventions of men who lived before me," he explained. "Let other men use mine."

Chapter *6*

Ben Flies Another Kite

When Ben was alive, electricity was a great mystery. No one knew much about it. But scientists all over the world were studying electricity. Ben was one of them.

Ben knew that lightning acted like electricity. But was it electricity? If Ben could only prove it!

Suddenly Ben had an idea. Perhaps he could prove that lightning was electricity by flying a kite during a thunderstorm. He knew that if lightning was electricity, it would travel down a wet kite string.

"William," he said to his son one summer day, "I want you to help me with an experiment. We must keep it a secret. People will laugh at us if it doesn't work."

Ben and his son made a kite out of a big silk handkerchief. They attached a wire to the frame. Ben thought the wire would attract lightning.

Neither Ben nor William knew it, but the experiment was very dangerous. If a strong lightning bolt struck the kite, they could be killed.

One dark and stormy day they took their kite to a field. William held the ball of string attached to the kite. Ben held the kite. He flung it into the wind and yelled "Go!"

William ran as fast as he could. At first, the kite wobbled from side to side. Then it rose gracefully into the air.

It was raining hard as Ben took the kite string from his son. They walked to a nearby shed. Ben tied a key to the end of the kite string.

The kite flew into a thundercloud. Lightning flashed about it. Thunder roared. But nothing happened.

"I'm afraid it's not going to work, Father," William said.

"Let's not give up yet," Ben answered.

Lightning flashed again. "Crack!" It struck the wire on the kite frame.

Suddenly the tiny threads on the kite string stood up straight. They were moved by an unseen force. Ben touched the key with his hand.

"Ouch!" he howled, taking his hand away quickly. "I got a shock! But we've proved it! Lightning *is* electricity!" He was lucky that the lightning which struck the kite was weak. Ben was not really hurt.

On their way home William said, "Now, Father, we have proved that electricity and lightning are the same. But what good is it?"

Ben smiled. "Knowing the truth is always good. And I am sure something good will come of our experiment. Just you wait and see."

Ben was right. Soon he thought of a way to protect houses from lightning. Lightning sometimes strikes houses. It can set them on fire.

Ben told the readers of his *Almanac* how to make lightning rods. He advised every man to put a metal rod on top of his house. The rod should be connected to the ground by a wire. When the lightning struck the rod, it would travel down the wire to the ground. The house would not be hurt. Lightning rods were put on many homes. Thanks to Ben, many lives were saved.

Ben's experiments with electricity were written about in Europe. He became famous all over the world. Many colleges gave him honorary degrees. From that time on, Ben was known as "Doctor Franklin".

Chapter 7

Ben Goes to England

Dr. Franklin was now the most important man in Pennsylvania. He was a member of the Pennsylvania Assembly. The Assembly was a group of men who made laws for the colony. But many laws were still made in England. They were made by the king and his group of lawmakers, the English Parliament.

One night Franklin came home from an Assembly meeting with exciting news.

"I must go to England very soon," he told Mrs. Franklin and Sally.

"Oh, Ben," Mrs. Franklin said, almost crying, "why must you go to England again?"

"The Assembly wants me to explain our problems to the King and Parliament. They don't understand what our problems are."

"May Mother and I go with you?" Sally asked.

"I hope so," her father answered. "William is too busy to come. I hate to go alone."

"No," Mrs. Franklin said. "Sally and I must stay here. The trip is too dangerous."

Franklin thought he would be gone for only a few months. But he had to stay in England ten years.

While he was in England, Parliament passed a law called the *Stamp Act*. It forced Americans to pay big taxes. The Americans were very angry.

"Americans are willing to pay taxes," Franklin told the English. "But only if the taxes are fair. We must be allowed to make the tax laws ourselves. You live too far away. You don't know what is right for America."

Franklin worked hard to get Parliament to end the Stamp Act.

"If the Stamp Act is not ended," he said, "Americans will stop buying English things. You will lose more money in trade than you would ever make in taxes."

The English knew he was telling the truth. Parliament repealed the Stamp Act.

When the news reached Philadelphia, the people were happy. "Hurrah for Ben Franklin!" they shouted.

Sally was proud of her father. She hoped he could come home. Sally had married William Bache. She wanted her father to meet him.

However, Franklin had to stay where he was. The troubles with England got worse. Parliament passed still another tax law. This one made the Americans even more angry.

"Why can't the English and Americans live in peace?" Franklin asked. "We can make the American laws. The English can make the English laws."

But the King and Parliament wanted to make the laws for both. As Franklin had told the Junto Club years before, "Even a king should listen to reason."

But King George III would not listen.

Franklin had done all he could. Just before he sailed for home, he had bad news from Philadelphia. His beloved Debbie was dead. And the love of the Americans for the English was dead too.

Franklin's homecoming was sad. But his heart filled with joy when he saw Sally and his two new grandsons. Their names were William and Benjamin Bache.

"Here is an English penny for each of you," Franklin told his grandsons. "Promise that you won't spend them on English things!"

The boys were happy when their famous grandfather moved into their house to live.

Chapter *8*

A New Job

War between America and England had begun while Franklin was on the ship coming home. The war was called the American Revolution.

Franklin had to go right to work to help his country plan the war. He was one of the leaders chosen to go to a meeting in Philadelphia.

At the meeting Franklin helped write the Declaration of Independence. It told the world that the American colonies were free and independent. No longer would they be ruled by unjust laws from England. The Declaration was passed on July 4, 1776.

When Franklin came home that night, he told his grandsons about the Declaration.

"What does it all mean?" William asked.

"It will mean a long war with England," Franklin said.

"Are you going to be a soldier, Grandfather?" Benny asked.

"I'm too old for that," Franklin answered, smiling.

But Franklin could help win the war in other ways. England was rich and powerful. America was poor and weak. The American leaders knew they must get help from France if they were to defeat the English. And they knew that the man to send for help was Franklin.

People would listen to his good ideas.

So once more Franklin sailed across the sea. His father had not let him be a sailor. But he was "going everywhere and seeing everything" just the same.

Franklin took two of his grandsons with him. Temple Franklin, William's son, was almost seventeen. Benjamin Franklin Bache was only seven. He was so gay that he made his grandfather feel young again.

They sailed on the *Reprisal.* One day Benny stopped the captain on deck. "Captain," he asked, "what will happen if the English capture our ship? Temple says they might hang our grandfather."

The captain laughed. "First they will have to catch up with us," he said.

"This is a fast ship. And if they catch up with us, we can probably capture them."

He was right. The *Reprisal* captured two English ships and took them to France. They were prizes of war. It was an exciting adventure for the boys.

Soon after they arrived in France, they moved into a nice house near Paris. Temple helped his grandfather with his work. Benny went to boarding school nearby.

Franklin became popular with the French people. He was so friendly and natural. The French liked his plain clothes and his old fur cap.

Sometimes Franklin was not well. He ached all over. So he would sit for hours in a bathtub of warm water.

The warm water made him feel better. But even when he felt sick, he kept on working. The bathtub had a cover on top. He asked important visitors to talk to him while he soaked in the bathtub!

And when he was well he went everywhere. The French people gave parties for him. Franklin was so popular that many families hung paintings of him in their homes. A picture of his face was put on medals and rings. Franklin wrote Sally that the pictures "have made your father's face as well known as that of the moon".

Chapter **9**

Winning the War

Franklin was very busy trying to get the French government to help America. At first the French were afraid to send soldiers to America. If they did, England might make war on France.

"I'll never give up," he told Temple. "France must help us win our freedom from the English."

Finally, after years of hard work, Franklin was successful. France agreed to help America win its war with England.

King Louis XVI of France invited Franklin to a big party at his palace.

The King was going to tell the world about the treaty of friendship the two countries had signed.

Temple said his grandfather must wear a wig to the palace. In those days all important men wore fancy wigs on top of their own hair.

"But I don't own a wig," Franklin said.

"I thought you would say that," Temple answered. "So I had one made."

Temple reached in a box and pulled out a wig. Franklin tried it on. The wig didn't fit.

"It's too little," Franklin said.

Just then a servant came into the room. "The wig is not too little, sir," he said. "But your head is much too big."

He meant that Franklin's head was so full of big ideas.

Franklin laughed. He went to the palace without a wig. Everyone who saw him said, "What a fine looking man!"

The King took Franklin by the hand. "I want you to tell the Americans how pleased I am with your work."

Even with France helping, the war went on and on. But one autumn day a ship from America brought wonderful news. American and French soldiers had captured the strongest English army in America. This meant the war would soon be over.

"Can't we go home now, Grandfather?" Benny asked.

"Not yet," Franklin said. "There is still work to be done."

"You've done as much work as ten men!" Benny said.

"I will never be through working for America," Franklin said. "We must stay in France until the peace treaty with England is signed."

When the peace treaty was finally signed, Franklin said, *"I hope we never see another war! There never was a good war or a bad peace."*

Chapter *10*

Waiting to Go Home

Before Franklin could go home, he had to wait for an American to take his place. Someone had to look after the new country's business in France.

During the years abroad, Franklin had never lost his interest in science. He was still curious about everything. He made experiments whenever he had a chance.

Now all Paris was excited about a new invention. It was a huge balloon that could carry a big basket up in the air. A rooster, a sheep and a duck had been sent up in the basket.

Now two brave men were going to try it. If they succeeded, they would be the first men to fly.

Franklin was as excited as the smallest boy. He took Benny out of school. They rode in a carriage to the park where the flight would take place.

The two brave men got into the basket. Other men untied the ropes that held the balloon down. What a thrilling sight it was when the balloon slowly rose in the air! The flyers waved. The people below all cheered and clapped.

"That's certainly better than any of my kites!" Franklin told Benny. "Perhaps the balloon will mean the end of war. Soldiers could be flown to enemy countries. Wars will get so terrible that maybe people will stop having them."

70

Franklin was enjoying his last months in Paris. He liked the French people. But still he longed to go home. He was old, and he was often sick. He wanted to see his family again.

At last, Thomas Jefferson arrived in Paris from America. He was to take over Franklin's work.

A Frenchman asked Jefferson, "Have you come to take Franklin's place?"

"I have come to succeed him," Jefferson answered. *"No one can take his place."*

Chapter *11*

Welcome Home

Franklin and his grandsons stood on deck as their ship sailed up the river toward Philadelphia.

Temple was twenty-five now. And Benny was a young man. But both were jumping up and down like children. Even Franklin was excited at seeing America after so long.

"You know, boys," Franklin said, "I rowed down this river when I first came to Philadelphia. I was seventeen years old then. And I didn't know anyone in Philadelphia."

Just then the ship came in sight of the city. Cannons started booming and church bells ringing.

"Look at the crowds standing on the riverbank!" Benny cried. "Why, they are waving and cheering!"

A passenger near them said, "Those people are there to welcome you home, Dr. Franklin."

"Times have changed, Grandfather," Benny said proudly. "Everyone in Philadelphia knows you now! You must be the most famous grandfather in all America!"

Franklin was pleased by his welcome. He had worked hard for his country. "Now," he thought, "I have earned a rest."

But America still had work for Franklin to do. America was a new nation. She needed a set of laws so the people could govern themselves.

Franklin was one of the leaders chosen to make the set of laws. The laws would be called *The Constitution of the United States of America.*

Though Franklin was very tired, he went to the meetings. The leaders talked about the laws for a long time. It was hard for them to agree on what was best for the people.

"No constitution can be perfect," Franklin told the men wisely. "But any constitution is better than none." He talked the other leaders into signing the Constitution. America is still governed by those laws.

Franklin was proud of the part he had played in his country's history. "I have helped build America," he said to himself. "My grandchildren will see it grow into a great nation."

Now Franklin could rest at last. He read books. He wrote letters to scientists. His friends and many grandchildren came to visit. Franklin was happy to see his favorite grandson, Benny, start a printing shop of his own.

Finally, in 1790, Benjamin Franklin died at the age of eighty-four.

But Franklin's name will live as long as America lives. Cities, counties, banks, a college and a great museum have all been named after the candlemaker's son from Boston.

You can see his picture on stamps and money. His face is still almost as "well known as that of the moon".

But Benjamin Franklin is best remembered for his ideas. His ideas helped make America a great nation.